TOTAL
VOLLEYBALL

BY ALEX MONNIG

SportsZone

An Imprint of Abdo Publishing
www.abdopublishing.com

abdopublishing.com

Published by Abdo Publishing, a division of ABDO, PO Box 398166, Minneapolis, Minnesota 55439. Copyright © 2017 by Abdo Consulting Group, Inc. International copyrights reserved in all countries. No part of this book may be reproduced in any form without written permission from the publisher. SportsZone™ is a trademark and logo of Abdo Publishing.

Printed in the United States of America, North Mankato, Minnesota
102016
012017

Cover Photos: Gwyneth Roberts/Lincoln Journal-Star/AP Images, foreground; Best Photo Studio/Shutterstock Images, background
Interior Photos: Best Photo Studio/Shutterstock Images, 1; Massimo Sambucetti/AP Images, 4–5; Kirby Lee/Long Beach Press-Telegram/AP Images, 6; AP Images, 8–9, 10, 13, 58–59; Andrea Crisante/Shutterstock Images, 14–15; Red Line Editorial, 15; Shutterstock Images, 16, 24, 27, 28–29; Aspen Photo/Shutterstock Images, 18–19; David Stluka/AP Images, 21; A. Lesik/Shutterstock Images, 22–23; Vladimir Pesnya/ Sputnik/AP Images, 31; Ronald Zak/AP Images, 32–33; Elaine Thompson/AP Images, 34; Bob Galbraith/AP Images, 37; Adam Butler/AP Images, 38–39; Misha Japaridze/AP Images, 41; David Goldman/AP Images, 42; Michael Spomer/Cal Sport Media/AP Images, 44–45; Daniel Ramalho/Rex Features/AP Images, 46; Sue Ogrocki/AP Images, 49; Nikki Carlson/Havre Daily News/AP Images, 50–51; Marcio Jose Sanchez/AP Images, 53; Beth A. Keiser/AP Images, 54–55; Cliff Schiappa/AP Images, 56; Joseph Sohm/Visions of America/Newscom, 61

Editor: Patrick Donnelly
Series Designer: Jake Nordby

Publisher's Cataloging-in-Publication Data

Names: Monnig, Alex, author.
Title: Total volleyball / by Alex Monnig.
Description: Minneapolis, MN : Abdo Publishing, 2017. | Series: Total sports |
    Includes bibliographical references and index.
Identifiers: LCCN 2016945679 | ISBN 9781680785081 (lib. bdg.) | ISBN
    9781680798364 (ebook)
Subjects: LCSH: Volleyball--Juvenile literature.
Classification: DDC 796.325--dc23
LC record available at http://lccn.loc.gov/2016945679

CONTENTS

KING KIRALY

Karch Kiraly was just 23 at the 1984 Olympics. But he showed the world why he would soon be known as the best volleyball player of all time.

Kiraly was the youngest member of the US men's national team at that year's Games. But he played perhaps the biggest role in the team's gold-medal success. His amazing passing skills gave US coach Doug Beal an idea. In those days, volleyball players didn't specialize as much on specific skills. For example, serves were received by anyone who could reach them. But Beal wanted his best passers to receive as many

Karch Kiraly sets the ball against Japan in the 1988 Summer Olympics.

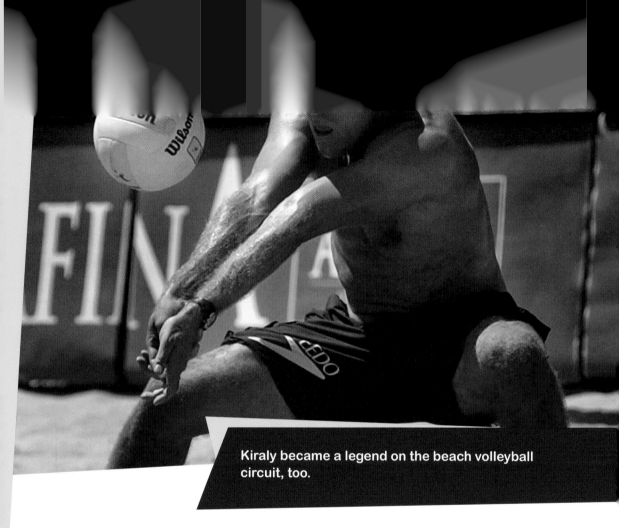

Kiraly became a legend on the beach volleyball circuit, too.

serves as possible. So he put Kiraly and teammate Aldis Berzins in charge of serve reception.

Kiraly's pinpoint passing was vital to the US attack as the team rolled to the gold medal in Los Angeles.

That was the beginning of a legendary career. Kiraly became US captain in 1985 and guided the team to the

1986 World Championship. Then he helped the United States win Olympic gold again in 1988. Kiraly was named the US team's Most Valuable Player (MVP) of the tournament.

Kiraly's success reached beyond the hard court. He is the winningest beach volleyball player of all time. He won gold on the beach at the 1996 Olympics in Atlanta, Georgia, with partner Kent Steffes. That made Kiraly the first to win indoor and beach volleyball gold at the Olympics. He ended his career with a record 148 beach titles.

The Fédération Internationale de Volleyball (FIVB) is the global governing body of the sport. It named Kiraly the best male player of the 20th century. One look at his commanding presence on the court makes it easy to see why.

SELF-SERVICE

Kiraly's phenomenal ball control led to plenty of great sets from his teammates, which in turn helped boost his ability as an attacker. "He was so easy to set because he would pass the ball perfectly every time. He'd practically set himself," said Mike Lambert, Kiraly's beach volleyball partner in 2004 and 2005.

2

EARLY
DAYS

Take the high-flying action of basketball. Mix it with a tennis net, but leave the rackets out. Throw in a bouncy ball made of leather. This combination is the result of the game invented by William G. Morgan in 1895.

Morgan was the director of physical education at the YMCA in Holyoke, Massachusetts. He taught physical fitness classes. It was his job to devise new sports and exercises. Morgan took pride in his work. His students appreciated him. Attendance in his classes boomed.

US troops in the South Pacific play volleyball inside a bombed-out church during World War II.

Morgan was a big fan of another new sport: basketball. He had met Dr. James Naismith in 1891. Naismith invented basketball at the YMCA in nearby Springfield, Massachusetts. Basketball was becoming more popular by the day. It involved intensity and physical contact. Those aspects were great for young students who needed rigorous but safe physical activity.

But Morgan's classes featured men and boys of various ages. Basketball was too difficult for the older men. He wanted to create a sport that was easy enough for middle-aged men to play during their lunch break.

EARLY RULES

Volleyball was initially called "mintonette." Many early rules were different from those used today. At first, teams could have as many players on the court as they wanted. Now each team can use only six players at a time. The first mintonette rules allowed teams to hit the ball as many times as they wanted before hitting it over the net. That is no longer the case. Now teams have three hits to return the ball.

Volleyball on the beach, 1943

So Morgan went to work. He wanted to use the best parts of basketball. And he wanted to employ them in a manner that suited everybody. Morgan also loved tennis and was inspired by that sport to use a net in his new game.

He set the top of the net to be 6 feet 6 inches (198 cm) off the ground. He thought that was just above the height of an average man. Then Morgan had a company make a special new ball for the game. Finally, he asked two friends to come up with the rules.

The Spalding sporting goods company manufactured the first volleyball.

Morgan debuted the sport on July 7, 1896, in a gymnasium at Springfield College in Springfield, Massachusetts. Two teams of five men lined up to play. Little did anybody realize how popular it would become. Morgan designed the game to be played indoors or outside. This helped spread its popularity

Team USA and Japan battle in the first Olympic women's volleyball tournament at the 1964 Tokyo Games.

to beaches and parks. US soldiers brought the game to Europe during World War I (1914–1918). During the 1920s, the United States created a national volleyball association.

3

POSITIONS AND ROTATIONS

Whether volleyball is played indoors or on the beach, it packs a lot of action into a relatively small playing space.

The court is a rectangle split into two halves by the net. The top of the net in a men's match is 7 feet 11 5/8 inches (2.43 m) off the ground. The net height is 7 feet 4 1/8 inches (2.24 m) for a women's match. These heights are the same for both indoor and beach matches.

The net cuts the indoor court into two squares. Each of these squares is 29 feet 6 inches (9 m)

The players on a volleyball court are referred to by numbers based on where they play.

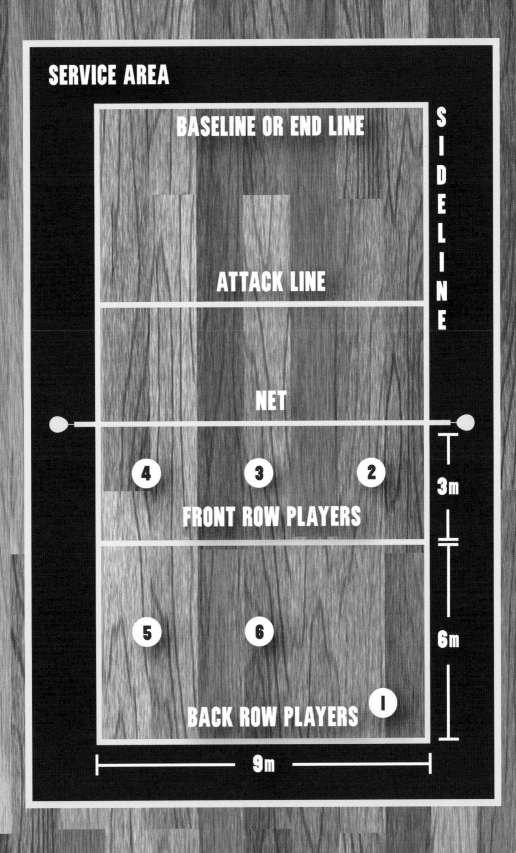

Beach volleyball is a lot simpler in concept than the indoor game.

per side. A line about 10 feet (3m) from the net on each side defines the attack area. Beach volleyball courts are a bit smaller at 26 feet 3 inches (8 m) per side. There is no attack line in the beach game.

An indoor team has six players on the court at a time. Players specialize in different positions. They must rotate clockwise to the next position once their team earns the serve back. This happens by scoring a point during a rally started by an opponent's serve.

The six spots on the court go by many names. Often they are referred to by the numbers 1 through 6. The server's spot is the position in the back right. It is No. 1. The rest of the positions are given numbers based on the serving order. Right front is 2, middle front is 3, and so on through 6.

THE NAME GAME

Many positions have multiple names. One example of this is the left front position. It is number 4. That player can also be called a pin hitter, an outside hitter, or a strong-side hitter. This player is often a team's best attacker and a strong passer of serves.

Beach volleyball is much simpler. There are two players on each team. They just have to alternate serving.

4

THE SCIENCE OF SETTING

Volleyball and football are very different sports. But both feature a player who is a clear-cut leader and has the greatest impact on the game. In football, it's the quarterback. In volleyball, it's the setter.

Fans love seeing a player leap high and smash the ball over the net. But that can't happen without a great set. The setter's job is to set up teammates to succeed and score points.

Ideally the setter takes every second ball. A teammate receives the serve and passes the

A good setter makes all of his or her teammates better.

SMALL PLAYERS, BIG SKILLS

Volleyball is a game for people of all sizes. Setter Josef Musil of the Czech Republic is one of the best setters ever. But he was not particularly tall. He stood only 5 feet 10 inches (179 cm). He also wasn't incredibly strong. He succeeded by perfecting his technique. He used his brains and technical ability to outsmart opponents. Musil led the Czech Republic to five World Championship medals and two Olympic medals in the 1950s and 60s.

ball toward the net. Passes are usually sent to an area between the middle attacker and the right front hitter. The setter should be there waiting for the ball.

The setter then passes the ball to a hitter. Setters reach their hands upward to meet the ball. They push the ball high above the net. That way a hitter can jump up and hit it down across the net.

But setters do much more than that. A setter calls plays for the team. This happens before each serve. It can also happen in the middle of the action. That means setters have to think quickly.

Each hitter can run different patterns when they approach to hit. Sometimes sets will

Setters can pass the ball to teammates who are in front of them or behind them.

be quicker. That means they are lower to the net. Other times sets are pushed to different areas of the net. This is all done to confuse the opposing defense. Setters alert teammates to special plays with hand signals or speaking in code. Setters are always trying to outthink the defense.

5

GETTING TACTICAL

Pass. Set. Hit. Volleyball can be a simple sport to learn. But it takes years to master.

Elite volleyball players are incredibly athletic. They fly high above the net and spike the ball at amazing speeds. They can also form a blocking wall at the net that's impossible to hit around. And they rely on their finely tuned reflexes to make spectacular diving saves. That means tactics are important. The tiniest advantages can make all the difference.

Volleyball players wow us with their spectacular athletic feats.

Tactics start at the serve. A serve is the first chance to attack an opponent. A tough serve often leads to a bad pass. And that sets off a chain reaction. A bad pass is tougher to set. A bad set makes it harder to attack. Some coaches will tell servers which opponent they should target with their serves. This is done to expose a weak passer on the other team.

Attacking tactics can be complicated. Blockers at the highest levels are giants. They can jump high enough to get their entire arms up over the net to block spikes. This makes it even more important to confuse them with strategy. This is a setter's primary job when calling plays. Many teams use combinations. These are plays in which hitters

QUICK TRICKS

The most common cog in a combination is the middle attacker. Setters will often have the middle attacker run a quick pattern. This is a set that is just over the height of the net. That makes the middle blocker commit to the middle hitter. This keeps the middle blocker from teaming up elsewhere on the net to block.

A strong serve can be tough to handle by even the best back-row players.

approach the net at different spots. The setter looks at the blockers and uses knowledge about the opposing defense to figure out which combinations will work best.

Complex tactics are used on defense as well. It's impossible for blockers to take away all of an attacking player's options. So they decide which part of the court to defend. They might attempt to block crosscourt hits. Or they might focus on blocking hits down the line. Blockers will communicate with defenders in the back row to let them know which part of the court they'll need to cover.

Concordia University (St. Paul, Minnesota) won seven straight Division II women's volleyball national titles (2007–2013).

The best teams can adapt their tactics during a match. Teams cannot keep doing the same thing on offense or defense. If they do, the opposition will start to catch on. Then they will change their own strategies and take advantage of it. That is why top teams are

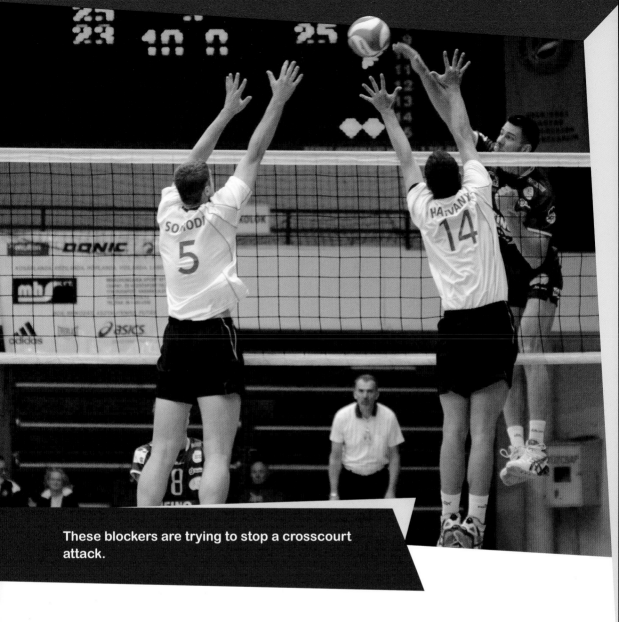

These blockers are trying to stop a crosscourt attack.

always changing who they target with their serves, which combinations they run, and how they set up their defense. Variety is not only more effective—it's more fun to watch players and teams try new tactics.

6

TOP COMPETITION

Volleyball is a global game. Several major competitions help determine which teams are the best. Every year teams from all over the world compete in two FIVB tournaments. The men compete in the World League, the women in the World Grand Prix.

The World League expanded to 36 teams in 2016. The World Grand Prix had 28 teams. Both have three levels of competition. Teams can move up and down these levels based on results in the

FIVB governs the most important volleyball tournaments in the world.

FIVB

OFFICIAL GAME BALL

previous year. The first World League event took place in 1990. The World Grand Prix began in 1993.

WHAT IS THE FIVB?

The FIVB is volleyball's governing body. It was founded in 1947. The FIVB is responsible for the biggest tournaments around the world. Its goal is to help grow the game. In 1993 the FIVB reached 210 member nations. That made it the largest sports organization in the world. That number sat at 221 in 2016.

Volleyball also has three tournaments that happen every four years. The men's World Cup started in 1965. The women's version started in 1973. Both are held in Japan. There are also men's and women's world championships every four years.

The world volleyball community also gathers every four years at the Summer Olympics. Men's and women's volleyball was added in 1964 and has been part of the event ever since.

The qualifying and early rounds for these competitions last for months. And the teams have to travel all over the world.

Team USA members celebrate after winning the 2015 FIVB men's World Cup in Tokyo.

So only one of these three major tournaments takes place each year.

Beach volleyball has major tours and tournaments. The FIVB hosts world championships every two years. The organization also runs an annual World Tour each year.

7 TOP TEAMS

Volleyball is one of the most popular sports in the world. Approximately 800 million people play it. Teams from many different countries have won the biggest tournaments. But a few teams stand out above the rest.

In men's volleyball, Brazil and Italy have been strong since the 1980s. The Italians ruled the 1990s and early 2000s. They stand as one of the greatest dynasties of all time. Coach Julio Velasco, middle blocker Andrea Gardini, and all-around stars Andrea Giani and Lorenzo Bernardi made them nearly unbeatable. Italy won three straight

Andrea Gardini, *left*, was a superstar for the Italian national team during its dominant run.

Cuba's Ana Ivis Fernandez, *left*, and Marlenis Costa team up to block Germany's Christina Schultz at the 2000 Olympic Games in Sydney, Australia.

World Championships and three Olympic medals. Italy also won a World Cup championship and eight World League titles from 1990 to 2000.

Brazil ended Italy's reign. The South Americans won three straight World Championships from 2002 to 2010. They also twice won gold (2004 and 2016) and silver (2008 and 2012) medals at the Olympics. Like the Italians, their success carried over to the World League.

Brazil won eight titles from 2001 to 2010. Coach Bernardo Rezende and outside hitter Gilberto Godoy Filho were two of the team's driving forces.

> **Brazilian duo Jackie Silva and Sandra Pires won the first gold medal in women's beach volleyball in 1996.**

On the women's side, Cuba dominated the 1990s. It was led by middle blocker Regla Torres. The team won three straight Olympic gold medals from 1992 to 2000. No other country had done that. They also won the 1994 and 1998 World Championships, the 1993 and 2000 World Grand Prix, and four straight World Cups from 1989 to 1999.

Four teams have often found themselves at the top of the women's game since Cuba's run ended. Brazil has had the most success since the turn of the century. The team won gold at the 2008 and 2012 Olympics. Brazil also captured seven World Grand Prix titles from 2004 to 2014.

Several countries have challenged Brazil's dynasty. Russia won the 2006 and 2010 World Championships. The United States won the 2014 World Championships and four World Grand Prix titles from 2010 to 2015. And China won gold at the 2004 and 2016 Olympics, 2003 and 2015 World Cup, and 2003 World Grand Prix.

The number of strong squads shows how the sport has truly become a global game.

Sandra Pires, *left*, and Jackie Silva defeated another team from Brazil to win the first beach volleyball Olympic gold medal.

8

QUEENS OF
THE BEACH

Misty May-Treanor turned her head to the left. She watched as the serve sailed out of bounds. She threw her arms in the air and went to hug US playing partner Kerri Walsh Jennings. The two had just won their third consecutive Olympic beach volleyball gold medal. It cemented them as one of the greatest beach volleyball duos in history.

May-Treanor and Walsh Jennings teamed up in 2001. That year they won their first tournament. They would win 103 more times during an amazing 11-year partnership.

Misty May-Treanor, *right*, celebrates with Kerri Walsh Jennings after they won their first Olympic gold medal.

The two won all 21 of their Olympic matches across the 2004, 2008, and 2012 Games. Even more impressive was their overall streak of 112 match victories from 2001 to 2008.

The partners balanced each other perfectly. That's because each played to her strengths. At 6 feet 2 inches (188 cm) Walsh Jennings was a powerful blocker. She started each play at the net. Her height and athleticism provided an imposing wall. May-Treanor was shorter, at 5 feet 8 1/2 inches (175 cm). She was quicker, too. So she played in the backcourt. It suited her well. May-Treanor relied on her strong passing skills to set up Walsh Jennings at the net. She also specialized in making outstanding digs.

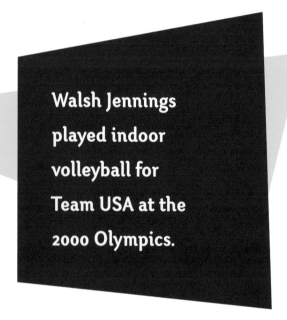

Walsh Jennings played indoor volleyball for Team USA at the 2000 Olympics.

The two players complemented each other in other ways, too. May-Treanor was quieter and had incredible focus.

Walsh Jennings makes a diving dig as May-Treanor prepares to make a play in a 2011 match.

Walsh Jennings was louder and more outgoing. Their personalities meshed seamlessly. This is especially important in a two-person team. They must act and play together as a unit at all times in order to be successful.

These traits added up to a lot of wins during their 11-year partnership. The duo won three straight World Championships (2005, 2007, and 2009) and was named Association of

Volleyball Professionals (AVP) Team of the Year five times in a row from 2003 to 2007.

It's hard to exaggerate the impact that May-Treanor and Walsh Jennings had on the sport. Interest in women's beach volleyball increased dramatically during their careers. The two spent countless hours running camps and clinics. They wanted to inspire the next generation of players to follow their sporting dreams.

PLAYING ON

Misty May-Treanor retired from beach volleyball after the 2012 Olympic Games. But Kerri Walsh Jennings was not finished. She earned a bronze medal with playing partner April Ross at the 2016 Olympics. Ross, along with her former partner Jennifer Kessy, lost to May-Treanor and Walsh Jennings in the final at the 2012 Olympics.

Their run ended with that final point at the 2012 Olympics. May-Treanor retired following the Games to start a family. Walsh Jennings later revealed she was five weeks pregnant with her third child during the 2012 Olympic final.

Walsh Jennings and Ross prepare to take the court at the 2016 Olympics.

9

CHANGING THE GAME

Volleyball's popularity grew fast in the latter half of the 20th century. But the game itself hadn't changed much. Members of the FIVB thought the sport needed to be more exciting. This way, more fans would watch on TV and sponsors would pay more money. So the FIVB introduced new rules.

One change adopted in 1998 created a new position. It is called the *libero*. The libero helps teams play better defense. Most middle blockers are tall, which makes them great in the front row. But they tend to be poor passers and defenders in the back row. So the FIVB introduced the libero.

US libero Kayla Banwarth passes the ball at the 2015 World Grand Prix finals.

Either team can score a point on a rally, not just the team that served.

The libero can play only in the back row. Liberos tend to be shorter. They are also agile. This makes them perfect players for the back row. They can make exciting defensive digs and pinpoint passes.

The innovations kept coming. Before 1999 teams could score points only when they served. But the FIVB wanted a point to be scored on every play. That made every rally equally important. So the organization introduced rally scoring. Now a team scores a point for winning a rally even if it did not serve.

Rally scoring meant that more points were being scored. So the FIVB increased the number of points needed to win a game. Winning teams in the past had to score 15 points. The FIVB changed that number to 25. Teams still have to win a game by at least two points.

The FIVB also decided to make a change to serving rules. Before 2000, a serve was not allowed to touch the net on its way over. Such a serve is called a let serve. Let serves resulted in

LIBERO LIMITATIONS

Liberos can be on the court at nearly all times. But there are rules to ensure that their primary impact is on defense. Liberos cannot attack the ball if it is above the net. That means they cannot block or spike. Liberos are also restricted in their setting. A front row attacker may not attack a ball if the libero overhead sets it from the front court.

side-outs. That meant no point was scored and the other team would serve.

More aggressive efforts, such as rocketed jump serves, were more likely to be let serves. The FIVB wanted to encourage players to unleash their hardest, most exciting serves. So it started allowing let serves. Now if a serve hits the net but crosses the center line, the point continues.

In 2016 Italy's Ivan Zaytsev tied an Olympic record by unleashing a serve at 79 miles per hour (127 km/h).

These new rules opened up a new era of volleyball. It has harder serves, thrilling defensive play, and intense, close matches.

Jump serves are less risky now that let serves are legal.

10

STAYING SAFE

Volleyball players fly through the air dozens of times each game. That means they hit the hard playing surface when they land. As a result, they need to take special care of their ankles and knees.

Taking off and landing puts stress on the legs. Players can also land awkwardly on another player's foot and roll an ankle. Ankle braces give extra support. Proper shoes can help, too. Volleyball shoes have gummy soles that provide more traction than a basketball shoe or other type of sneaker. That means you can count on more consistent takeoffs and landings. If you have a pair

Proper gear, such as knee pads, ankle braces, and shoes, can help protect you from injuries.

CUSHIONED COURTS

Indoor volleyball was originally played on gym floors. Now major tournaments use special floors. They can be laid over traditional surfaces. These courts are made of a spongier material. It is more forgiving than hardwood gym floors. That makes it safer for players' joints.

of shoes that fit properly and stay tied, you shouldn't have to worry about slipping and sliding around the court.

Staying low is key in the back row. An average spike travels 70 to 80 miles per hour (113 to 129 km/h). Every millisecond is vital. So players dive and roll on the floor to keep the ball in the air on defense. Padded knee guards protect players from bruises and floor burns. Some players also wear padded shorts to cushion their hips. This extra padding gives players confidence to make digs that they otherwise might not attempt.

On the beach, players should wear sunscreen to protect their skin. A visor will keep the sun out of a player's eyes. And most competitors wear eye protection. Sports shades

Many beach volleyball players wear eye protection, even at night, to keep sand out of their eyes.

are preferable to fashion sunglasses, as they're made to be shatterproof. They also provide more coverage to help protect the eyes from sand and other debris.

TERRIFIC TORRES

Cuban middle blocker Regla Torres took two steps to her right. She took off from her left foot near the right-side hitter's zone. The 6-foot 3-inch (191-cm) Torres leapt. She swung her right arm and smashed the ball down the line. Cuban players, coaches, and fans erupted. The team had just come back from a 2–0 deficit against Russia to win its third straight Olympic gold medal. No team had won gold in women's volleyball at three consecutive Games before.

That 2000 gold medal is one the most memorable moments in Torres's stellar career.

Regla Torres powers the ball past two defenders at the 2000 Olympics.

She was chosen as the top women's player of the 20th century by the FIVB. One look at her résumé explains why.

Torres burst onto the scene at the 1992 Olympics. She was just 17 years old. Cuba's win made her the youngest player ever to win a volleyball gold medal at the Games. Torres's height and quickness made her an amazing middle blocker. Her defense was key to Cuba's victory.

But Torres also excelled in other aspects of volleyball. Many middle blockers are bad at receiving serves. But Torres earned the titles of Best Receiver and MVP at the 1993 World Grand Prix. She was also named Best Receiver at that year's World Grand Champions Cup. She was named Best Blocker at the 1994 and 1998 World Championships, Best Server at the 1998 BCV Volley Masters tournament, and Best Spiker at the 2000 Olympics.

In addition to the three Olympic titles, Torres guided Cuba to triumphs at the 1994 and 1998 World Championships and the 1995 and 1999 World Cups.

Torres celebrates Cuba's gold medal at the 1992 Olympics.

12

HONORING THE GREATS

William G. Morgan invented volleyball in Holyoke, Massachusetts. So it makes sense that Holyoke would be the home of the International Volleyball Hall of Fame (IVHF).

The IVHF opened its doors to the public in 1987. At first only US players, coaches, and other important figures were considered for inclusion. That changed in 1998, when the IVHF started including international players. This gave the hall of fame its true global flavor.

Flo Hyman, former captain of the US women's team, was inducted into the IVHF in 1988.

THE FIRST INDUCTEE

The IVHF is full of players with huge vertical leaps, amazing quickness, and silky-smooth setting hands. They have combined to win hundreds of medals in the biggest competitions. But none can claim to be the first IVHF inductee. That honor goes to William G. Morgan, the game's inventor. Morgan, who died in 1942, was inducted in 1985, two years before the building itself opened.

The nomination policies are strict. A person must be retired from the position for which he or she is considered. The person must have spent at least 10 years in the position. And the person must have achieved significant recognition, such as playing for or coaching a national team, winning national or international competitions, or being selected for international honors.

The museum includes exhibits that honor the inductees and illustrate the history of the sport. Olympic volleyball, beach volleyball, college volleyball, the FIVB, and volleyball in the military each have dedicated space at the museum.

Two fans check out a US Olympic team display at the IVHF.

Including the 2015 class, 125 players, coaches, and leaders from 21 countries have been inducted into the IVHF. This variety shows how much the game has grown since its birth in the late 19th century.

GLOSSARY

approach
The movements made before jumping and hitting the ball.

attack
When a player tries to score a point by hitting the ball over the net toward the opponent.

attack line
A line on the floor that runs parallel to the center and end lines on both sides of the court. It is 3 meters (almost 10 feet) from the net and separates each side into a front zone and back zone.

libero
A ball-control specialist who plays only in the back row and wears a different-colored jersey.

match
An entire volleyball contest, which is made up of three to five sets or games. The first team to win three sets is the winner.

rally
The series of actions two teams make to keep the ball in play. When a rally ends, one team is awarded a point.

side-out
A play that ends with the serving team losing the point.

spike
A hard-driven ball from a player's overhead swing that lands in the opponent's court.

FOR MORE INFORMATION

Books

Ackerman, Jon. *Make Me the Best Volleyball Player*. Minneapolis, MN: Abdo Publishing, 2017.

Doeden, Matt. *Volleyball*. Mankato, MN: Amicus, 2015.

Forest, Anne. *Girls Play Volleyball*. New York: PowerKids Press, 2016.

Websites

To learn more about volleyball, visit **booklinks.abdopublishing.com.** These links are routinely monitored and updated to provide the most current information available.

INDEX

ABOUT THE AUTHOR

Alex Monnig is a freelance journalist from St. Louis, Missouri, who now lives in Sydney, Australia. He graduated with his master's degree from the University of Missouri in 2010. During his career he has covered sporting events around the world and has written more than a dozen children's books.